CHARLES FERRO

AF238565

HORROR

AT

REMSEN HIGH

In memory of Jim Kenner

Illustrations: Don Johnson

Charles Ferro:
Horror at Remsen High
Teen Readers, Level 3

Cover layout: Mette Plesner

Cover photos: ArminStautBerlin/iStock, hudiemm/iStock

Series editors: Ulla Malmmose
and Charlotte Bistrup

Editorial consultants:
Margaret Kersten, KLETT
Catherine Candea, BORDAS
Annemarie Zinck, ASCHEHOUG DANSK FORLAG A/S
Ulla Malmmose, ASCHEHOUG DANSK FORLAG A/S

ISBN Denmark 978-87-23-54237-3
www.easyreader.dk
The CEFR levels stated on the back of the book
are approximate levels.

Easy Readers
EGMONT

Printed in Denmark

About the author

Charles Ferro was born in Utica, a medium-sized city in upstate New York. He holds a Bachelor of Business Administration degree from St. John Fisher College, and earned a certificate for the teaching of English at the State University of New York. Currently employed as finance editor at the Danish news agency, Ritzaus Bureau.

Charles Ferro has been living in Denmark since 1977 with his wife Rita. They have a daughter, Maria Celeste. Charles enjoys reading, fishing and cooking.

When he was around nine years old, he asked his grandmother to take him to af movie made from an Edgar Allan Poe story. Since then he has loved stories about the supernatural.

About writing Charles Ferro says, "Part of my brain is still fourteen years old and doing books for kids is an excellent means of reliving part of my life - things that did happen and lies about what never happened."

1

Jake looked at himself in the mirror, but all he could see was the large red *pimple* that had grown on his cheek. He never got pimples, well almost never, and this one was a prizewinner. Of course it came at the worst time. In just one hour Jake would be in Biology class, next to 5 Suzy Monohan, the prettiest girl in school. In sixteen years he had only had around a dozen pimples, and now this.

His mother had stopped him from *squeezing* it. She said it was not ready yet, and squeezing would only 10 make it worse. His father suggested that Jake cover it with a *plaster*. He did not think that was funny. Jake became very angry when his mother said she would put some make-up on it.

No. He couldn't squeeze it, he couldn't go out with 15 a plaster on his cheek, and he would never wear make-up. But he couldn't walk into Remsen High School with a Christmas-tree light on his cheek either. Maybe he could wear a plaster and say he cut himself shaving, except nobody would believe he needed to shave just 20 under his right eye. In fact he only shaved twice a week.

Jake looked at the pimple, big, round and red. It did not hurt, even though it was so big. Squeeze it, he thought, that was the thing to do, even if he had to use

---

pimple, a red spot, usually on the face, common among teenagers
squeeze, press between two fingers
plaster, a strip of material to cover a sore or a pimple

a pair of *pliers*. Then he could wash it around twenty times until it dried out.

He walked out of the bathroom and to his own room. Before going in he stopped for a second to look at the
5 sign on his bedroom door. "JAKE WINSLOW" was burned into a piece of wood. Jake had made it in school four years ago when he was twelve. It should say "JAKE WINSLOW, PIMPLE KING", he thought as he walked into his bedroom.

10 The clock on the wall said it was 7:42. In 58 minutes Biology class would start and there he would sit with the world's biggest pimple on his cheek.

Jake fell onto his bed, rolled over on his back and looked at the ceiling. With one finger he began drawing
15 circles around the *lump* on his cheek. It *tickled*, but it did not hurt. Jake took his finger away from his cheek, but it felt as if something was still touching it. He waited a couple of seconds for it to stop. Instead the feeling became stronger, like something was pushing from in-
20 side his skin.

Jake jumped off the bed and walked to the mirror. His heart *pounded* when he saw that his cheek was moving. The skin under his eye moved up and down, and the pimple had grown bigger.

25 What Jake saw next made him want to scream. He saw a green spot where the pimple was. The spot grew larger and there was an orange color too. Something was coming out of his skin.

---

lump, thick part of a thing's surface
tickle, touch someone to make them laugh
pound, hit hard

pliers (pair of)

He took a step back and watched as a hairy, black leg came out. The leg moved on his cheek like an arm reaching for something. Jake saw a second leg, then a third. The orange and green spot grew larger every second. He could not feel it, but could see that something was trying to crawl out of his skin.

Jake jumped back from the mirror as he watched a green and orange thing pop right out of his cheek. His heart stopped beating. He looked downwards until he could see his nose. Jake could see something on his right cheek, and he could feel it moving.

The mirror showed a creature standing on three hairy black legs. Its green body was about two centimeters long with black and orange spots. The green-black head turned to look around the room with two shiny black eyes, stopping to look into Jake's eyes. The thing looked like it was half *ladybug* and half *spider*.

Jake reacted quickly. He tried to hit the thing with his right hand. The hand struck his cheek with a *SLAP*. He slowly took his hand from his face to see if he had killed the creature. There was nothing on his hand and nothing on his cheek. It had got away.

He looked around the room. The thing stood on the clock looking at Jake. The boy moved slowly to the bed and took a *pillow*. He took one step toward the clock on

---

slap, hit with open hand, or the sound this makes
pillow, something you put under your head when you sleep

ladybug

spider

the wall and swung the pillow at it. The clock crashed to
the floor, but Jake missed the creature. It stood on the
desk, looking back at Jake. When Jake moved again,
the thing ran across the desk and jumped to the floor. It
5 ran on its three legs and hid under the bed.

Jake bent over to look under the bed, but for a few
seconds he did not know why he was looking. Then he
recalled the green-orange creature, but the thought was
far far away in his mind. He sat on the bed and didn't
10 know what to do next when his mother opened the door.
"What was that noise?" she asked, but at the same time
saw his cheek. "Did you squeeze that pimple?"

"No," he said. "Something came out of it. A spider

or some kind of insect came out by itself." The words sounded like a lie even to Jake.

She *grabbed* his chin and inspected his cheek. "Nonsense. Spiders don't come out of people's faces. You squeezed the pimple and now you have a red mark on 5 your face."

"But Mom, it's true. I . . ." He did not know what to say. It felt as if something was taking away his memory.

"Come on, Jake, stop that nonsense. I don't want to hear it," she said. He could see that she would never 10 believe the truth, but now he wasn't even sure it was the truth.

She looked at the broken clock on the floor and then at him. "Is anything wrong?" she asked.

Jake tried to stay calm, although he started to feel 15 sick. "No." he lied.

She looked again at the broken clock on the floor and then back at Jake. "Well, I didn't like that clock anyway," she said. "Now hurry up and get ready for school or you'll be late." She went out and closed the door 20 behind her.

Jake took some deep breaths and waited a few seconds. Then he got down on his hands and knees to look under the bed. Nothing was there. He did not believe what he had seen . . but he had seen it, hadn't he? 25 Jake was no longer sure. It felt as if he was waking up from a dream. The pictures, inside his head, of a green-orange creature were like an old memory. He could remember something, but not all the details.

He thought for a moment and then went to the mir- 30 ror. There was a tiny red + on his cheek where the

---

grab, take hold of something quickly and firmly

"pimple" had been. There was no blood. It did not hurt when Jake touched the mark. Maybe it really had not happened. But it seemed that something had *hatched* from his face, just like a chicken from an egg. Jake got
5 down and looked under the bed again. Nothing.

"Jake," his mother called. "Hurry up or you'll be late."

He jumped to his feet, looking at the wall to see the time, and then at the broken clock on the floor. He
10 would be late for school if he didn't hurry. He put on his jacket and thought, "Maybe some insect fell from the ceiling onto the pimple and..." That was what he wanted to believe, but at the same time he could not understand what had happened. The memory was like
15 an old *faded* photograph. The pimple probably burst by itself, he decided, but...

Jake was still wondering about what had happened as he left for school. Had something happened, or had it been a dream? "Just to be sure, I'll look for that thing
20 when I get home--if it's really there," he said to himself.

---

hatch, come out of an egg, for example a baby bird
faded, having lost its color

2

Jake thought about what had happened as he walked to school. All he could remember was that something strange had happened, but he could not really remember exactly what. Inside his head, he could see pictures of something green and orange, with hairy black legs. He did not know what it was. He remembered throwing a pillow at the wall and breaking his clock.

The morning sun shining on his face helped him think about other things. After a few minutes he met his friend Bobby Rockla and the two walked together.

Jake and Bobby met at the same place every day. They usually talked quite a bit. Bobby and Jake would talk about girls, sports, school and summer vacation that was only a month away. But today both boys had little to say. Bobby kept running his right hand through his red hair and down the side of his face.

As they walked into the school, Bobby turned to Jake and said: "I have to go get my Biology book. I'll meet you in class."

Jake started to say something, but stopped. There was a red + on Bobby's right cheek. Jake felt fear tickle his heart. It was exactly like the one Jake had on his cheek. He knew the mark meant something, but he couldn't remember what.

Bobby turned to walk away and Jake said: "See you later," in a weak voice. What did the red + on Bobby's face mean? The thought *bothered* Jake, but he did not

---

bothered, worried by something

know why. He touched his own cheek, where he had a mark. He remembered a pimple, but..that was not unusual.

"Hi, Jake," Suzy Monohan said from behind him.
5 "We'd better hurry or we'll be late for Biology class."

Jake forgot about Bobby when he saw the pretty blonde girl. "Hi," he said with a big smile. They walked to Biology class together.

Suzy sat down and Jake took the seat next to her.
10 They talked for a minute until the bell rang. Then Mr Damick, the Biology teacher, started talking about *bio-technology* and *genetic engineering*. Jake looked around the room. He heard the teacher's voice, but not his words. Something seemed to be different about the class. It
15 was too quiet.

Jake looked at the faces of the others. Some of them looked worried or afraid. Jake's ears became hot when he saw the red + on Leo Manin's right cheek. Leo sat stiff in his chair and his eyes looked into empty space.
20 Jake looked at others. There was a red + on Joe Lamman's cheek too, and one on Robert Zoe's, as well, and...

"Jake, do you want to open your book, or would you rather look around the room?" Mr Damick asked.

25 Jake turned in his seat and opened the book. His heart beat in his throat. He was filled with terror. Every time he saw a red + on someone's cheek, his heart beat harder and faster. What did it mean? He felt as if he was

---

bio-technology, science that studies living things to find new uses for these
genetic engineering, science that tries to change living things, sometimes by mixing two living things

supposed to remember something that had happened. What was it?

He sat there with the book in front of him, but all he saw was the colors green and orange in front of his eyes. Mr Damick's voice continued, but Jake did not hear a word. After a few minutes he began to look around the room again. Every few seconds he would look back at his book so the teacher would think he was following the lesson.

Jake counted. There was Bobby Rockla: he had a little red + on his right cheek. And there were four other boys who had the same little red marks on their right cheeks. He could not see the faces of those who sat in front of him and only the left cheeks of those who sat to his right. Jake looked at his book again and started thinking. He had not seen any marks on any of the girls faces.

He looked around again. In the back of the room, Jim Murphy sat touching his right cheek with a finger. Jim looked puzzled. There was a large red pimple on Murphy's cheek! Jake turned back to his book. His stomach felt large and empty. It was as if the room was *spinning*. He wanted to turn around again to look at Jim Murphy, but he was too terrified. Why?

Jake sat looking at the pages of the book when he heard the scream. He turned just in time to see Jim Murphy jumping from his seat.

"IT JUMPED OUT OF MY FACE! AN ORANGE THING JUMPED OUT OF MY FACE!" Murphy screamed. The boy was out of his seat

---

spin, go round and round

and pointing at the floor. There was a green-orange
spot on the floor. It looked as if someone had spilled a
few drops of pea soup there.

"I killed it!" Murphy cried. "It jumped out of my
5 face and I killed it!"

Mr Damick walked quickly to Murphy. Some of the
other pupils stood up to look at Murphy and the spot on
the floor. "Sit down and read the rest of the chapter,"
the teacher said. "I'll be back in a minute." He took
10 Jim Murphy by the arm and said, "You come with me.
We're going to the office to call your parents. Are

14

you on drugs, Murphy? Animals don't jump out of people's faces. You're in trouble."

Jim Murphy was still trying to tell about the animal he had killed as Mr Damick took him from the room.

Some of the pupils in the room began to read their books. A few talked and laughed with each other and a few stood around the green spot on the floor. "Murphy spit on the floor," one of the girls said. The others laughed. "Murphy probably didn't want to sit and listen to Mr Damick talking for forty-five minutes about bio-engineering," another girl said. "So he spit on the floor and started shouting." Jim Murphy was known to be a clown.

"But now he'll get in trouble for drugs," Suzy Mono-han said. The teachers were always warning the kids about drugs. Schools in big cities had drug problems, but not here in Remsen.

"He doesn't take drugs," a boy said. "He'll just get into trouble for spitting on the floor. But I'll bet you anything Mr Damick will give a talk on the dangers of drugs when he comes back."

Jake's memory started to come back to him. He remembered standing in his bedroom, and something green and orange coming out of his face. He could now recall most of what had happened in his bedroom an hour earlier, but not everything.

Jake looked at the other boys who had red +'s on their cheeks. Four of them sat at their desks without saying a word. It looked as if they had each seen a ghost. Leo Manin stood by the spot on the floor and just stared at it. He didn't talk with the others. Jake stood up and walked over to Leo.

Leo looked at Jake and saw the red + on his face.

15

Neither boy said anything. Wilbur Ericsson came and stood next to Jake a few seconds later. Jake looked at Wilbur. He was the best student in class and probably the smartest in the whole school. Wilbur never played
5 sports and always seemed to have his nose in a book. Many of the other boys liked to *tease* Wilbur and laugh at him, because he was not very big and was so smart. Jake and his friends didn't spend a lot of time with Wilbur, but they didn't tease him either. Wilbur also
10 had a little red + on his cheek.

"We must talk after class," Wilbur said to Jake and Leo. "And some of the other boys, too." Leo looked at Wilbur, saw the mark on his cheek and nodded his head. "The same thing has happened to us all. I think
15 we should do something about it."

Wilbur, Leo and Jake moved away from the group of boys and girls that stood talking. Leo started to say something when Mr Damick walked back into the room with a paper towel in his hand.

20 "All right, let's get back in your seats," the teacher said. He waited at the side of the room until everyone was seated. Then he went over to the spot on the floor and cleaned it up with the paper towel. He threw the paper in the waste basket and walked to his desk at the
25 front of the room. "You all know that drugs are bad for you. Now you have seen what they can do. I don't think I need to say any more." Mr Damick sat down and opened his book.

Jake looked at Leo, then at Wilbur. The three of
30 them waited for the bell to ring.

---

tease, make fun of someone, sometimes in a bad or cruel way

16

3

Wilbur walked quickly out of the room when the bell rang. Leo Manin was standing by his side when Jake walked out of the room. The three stopped Joe Lamman, Robert Zoe, and Bobby Rockla. All six boys had red +'s on their cheeks. Joe, Robert and Bobby seemed to know why the other three asked them to stop.

After a few seconds Wilbur said: "Some kind of creature jumped out of our cheeks today. Right?" It wasn't often they talked to Wilbur Ericsson. For one thing, he was so smart it was hard to understand what he talked about. Another thing was that Wilbur was teased so often in school that he avoided the other students.

"What was it?" Robert Zoe asked.

"I don't know, but I have some ideas," Wilbur said. "I remembered that something had happened to me this morning, something scary, but I could not remember what it was. It felt as if I had got a shot of *novocain* in my brain. When Jim Murphy shouted and I saw that dead thing on the floor, I could remember everything. It was like suddenly being able to remember a dream. Did you feel the same way?"

The other boys all nodded their heads.

Wilbur took a paper out of his bookbag. "Look at this," he said. The five others stood in a circle around him.

Wilbur pointed at some words and numbers on the paper. "Some kind of animal was in our bodies, ours

---

novocain, medicine the dentist uses so you won't feel anything

and Jim Murphy's too. Why did it happen to us?" Wilbur said, not expecting an answer. Leo started to ask a question, but Wilbur held up a finger to silence him. He continued: "There are twenty-seven pupils in
5 the class. Fourteen girls and thirteen boys. Seven of us have red marks on our cheeks. None of the girls has the mark."

"Is it only boys? What about others in school?" Jake asked.

10 "I have looked at many others in school and I have only seen red marks on us. Now, we are boys, and we are in the same class," said Wilbur. "And..." He stopped to look at each of them. "We all have brown eyes."

15 "Do you mean all the brown-eyed boys in our class had a green and orange thing jump out of their cheeks?" Robert Zoe asked.

"Almost all of them," Wilbur answered. "August Brennan has brown eyes, but no red mark on his
20 cheek."

"What does that mean?" Robert asked.

"I don't know," Wilbur answered. "Have any of you an idea what it could mean?" Nobody said a word. It surprised them that Wilbur would ask them a question,
25 but they had no answers anyway.

"I think we should leave school and make a plan," Wilbur said. All the others were surprised he said this. Wilbur never even missed a class. Now he suggested they skip school. "We must try to find out what these
30 things are...and what they do." He looked at the others. They all nodded their heads to say they would do it.

"Did any of you tell your parents or anybody else?"

18

Wilbur asked them.

"My mother had already gone to work," Leo said.

"My parents too," Robert added.

"I couldn't remember what had happened until just a few minutes ago," Bobby told them. "Same here," 5 Joe said. "I tried to tell my mother, but she didn't believe it," Jake said. "And then the memory of it disappeared."

"Where are those things..those animals now?" Leo asked. "Mine ran under my desk and I couldn't find 10 it."

"Mine ran into the *closet*," Bobby added.

"Mine ran..." Robert began, but Wilbur held up his hand.

"All of yours ran away somewhere and hid, right?" 15 Wilbur asked. The others nodded. "And we saw Murphy kill one." Again the boys nodded. "But I caught mine." Wilbur said. The stared at him with their mouths hanging open. "I was brushing my teeth. I felt something moving in my cheek, so I looked in the 20 mirror and saw when it started to come out." Wilbur explained. The other five felt cold *shivers* run up the backs of their legs as they remembered that the same thing had happened to them. "There is a glass in our bathroom. I caught the thing in the glass." Nobody 25 could speak. "I put it in with my *turtle*. I thought Speedy would eat the thing. And then I too forgot all about

---

closet, small cupboard or room to keep clothes
shiver, shake either because you are cold or frightened

turtle

it." Wilbur's face was white as a dead man's foot. He *swallowed*. "I can remember that the creature was looking at me. It looked right into my eyes."

The six were silent for several seconds, as each
5 remembered his own experience with the horrible creatures.

"I think we should go over to my house," Wilbur said. "Maybe the creature is still there. If so, we can study the thing and try to find some ideas about what it
10 is, and what it will do."

"Why couldn't we remember anything, before we saw what happened to Murphy?" Jake asked.

"I don't know," Wilbur answered. "Maybe the things put some kind of poison in us, or maybe it was
15 such a shock seeing those things that our brains made us forget."

"Let's go then," said Robert Zoe. "Maybe we can get some answers."

"Come on," Leo said, and started to walk away.
20 Jake took Leo by the arm. "Wait," he said. "We can't all walk out together. Someone will see us. We can go out two at a time and meet down at the corner of Elm and High streets. Leo, you and Bobby go now, then Robert and Joe, and Wilbur and I will follow."

25 The bell rang and the other kids in school began to go to their next class.

"OK, let's get going," Leo said and walked toward the door with Bobby Rockla. Joe and Robert went in the other direction, toward the back door.

30 Jake and Wilbur waited a minute and then went out

---

swallow, allow (food, drink, etc) to pass down the throat to the stomach

20

the front door.

"I'm afraid," Wilbur admitted.

"You're not alone," Jake answered.

4

Wilbur unlocked the front door to his house as the others waited behind him. They entered the house and followed Wilbur up the stairs. "My room is at the end," he said, and walked that way, the others right behind
5 him. They were all anxious to see one of the things that had hatched from their cheeks.

Wilbur opened the door to his room and went over to the meter-long glass cage where the turtle lived. He switched on the light above the turtle's cage and bent
10 over to look through the glass. Wilbur jumped back and cried, "Speedy!"

Jake went to the cage and looked in. There were a few plants, some stones and a dish of water inside the cage. He saw Speedy at the right side of the cage. The turtle
15 lay on its back. Except there was no more turtle, only an empty shell. The head, tail, body and legs were all gone.

Jake looked at Wilbur. His mouth was open, but no words could come out. Wilbur was pointing at the left
20 side of the cage. Jake followed Wilbur's finger and saw what filled the other boy with fear. At first Jake thought it was a stone, but then he saw the orange spots. The animal that had jumped out of Wilbur's face stood in a corner of the cage. It looked at Jake, then at Wilbur. Its
25 head turned from one to the other. Jake could feel the eyes looking coldly into his own.

The creature had eaten the turtle, and now it was as big as one of Jake's shoes. The thing stood on two of its three legs. Its head was almost the size of a tennis ball.
30 It kept turning to look at Jake and Wilbur. Joe, Robert,

Bobby and Leo came up beside the other two.

"I don't believe it," Leo said. He took a step back from the cage.

"It's...it's...big!" Bobby whispered.

Jake looked at Wilbur again. Tears rolled down his cheeks. "Speedy was my only friend," Wilbur said. "Now he's dead."

Jake put an arm around Wilbur's shoulder and said, "Sit down for a minute. It will be all right." He led Wilbur to the bed and sat there with him. "Wilbur, we need your help. You know a lot of things. Maybe we can find out what they are, and...you can find a way to...to kill these things."

Wilbur took off his glasses and dried his eyes. The other boys came over to the bed and stood around Jake and Wilbur. Leo said: "Let's kill it and go get the others."

"Do you want to open the cage and do it?" Robert Zoe asked. Leo thought about the question for a second and answered: "No".

"Leo's right," Wilbur said. "We don't know what would happen if we opened the cage. It might jump out. And maybe it would go after one of us." The boys trembled in fear at the thought. Wilbur continued, "First we must find out what it is, and then we will find a way to kill it. Right now I'm only sure of one thing: there are not any animals or insects that look like that." He pointed at the cage. All the boys looked at the green-orange thing in the cage and it looked right back at them.

"Let's get out of here and talk," Leo said. "I don't like that thing looking at me."

"Good idea," Wilbur said. "Let's go down to the

kitchen." He turned to look at the dead turtle and more tears came to his eyes. They waited for Wilbur outside his room. When he came out a minute later, they followed Wilbur downstairs to the kitchen. The others sat around the table while Wilbur took six Coca-Colas from the refrigerator. 5

For fifteen minutes they talked. What they knew was that the thing looked like a spider and a ladybug. However, at the same time it didn't look like either insect. And they knew that it ate meat, and it grew fast. 10 Both spiders and ladybugs ate meat, Wilbur told them. But they usually ate insects that were much smaller. Even Wilbur could not understand how such a little thing could have eaten the turtle. Speedy was ten times as big as it was. 15

Then the boys started to talk about why it had happened to them and not any of the others. "We all have brown eyes, and Jim Murphy has too," Joe Lamman said. "But why us? There are a lot of other boys in school with brown eyes. Why didn't it happen to them 20 too?"

"It must be just our class then," Jake said. "But why us?"

"And what about August Brennan," Joe said. "He has brown eyes, but he did not have a red mark on his 25 cheek."

"That's it!" Wilbur said and jumped out of his chair. "August didn't go with the class to New World Bio-Laboratories last week."

"You're right. He didn't. He was sick that day," Jake 30 agreed. "But what do you mean?"

"Brennan has brown eyes, but it didn't happen to him," Wilbur said. "Because he wasn't at New World that day. Don't you see? At New World they do work with bio-technology and genetic engineering. They try to make new kinds of plants and even animals. Scientists take something from the *cells* of one type of living thing and put it into the cells of another. It makes a new animal or plant. They did it with oranges and found a new kind of orange that won't be hurt by cold. That's just one example."

"Do you think that some kind of new animal got into us. Is that what you are trying to say?" Robert asked.

"Yes!" Wilbur answered.

"But why us?" Jake asked. "Even if you are right...why us?"

"Who knows? Maybe the bodies of fifteen or sixteen-year old boys are just right for this kind of...of new animal. Maybe we have chemicals in our bodies that are perfect for carrying an egg, or whatever it was that was in us. Some spiders do lay eggs in other animals. And flies lay eggs in the bodies of dead animals," Wilbur said.

"Flies lay eggs in dead animals so the maggots, those little white worms, have something to eat when they hatch," Leo said. He did not know a lot about biology, but he was proud of what he did know.

"It didn't hurt when it came out. It found a way to get into us and then out again. We didn't even know they were there until they came out. The thing must be intelligent, or else it knows how to survive." Wilbur stopped and the others waited for him to say more. "It ate Speedy. Maybe this is some kind of new animal they

---

cell, the smallest part of a living thing

26

have created at New World. If it could eat a turtle that was much bigger than it was, what else can it do?"

"I don't like this at all," said Leo.

"I have an idea," Wilbur said. "Maybe we can learn some more from New World. Come on upstairs. I'm going to call them." The boys ran up the stairs behind Wilbur. There was a telephone on a small table in the hall. Wilbur took the telephone book to find New World Bio-Laboratories' number. He found it and pushed the numbers on the telephone.

Jake took a few steps back and looked into Wilbur's bedroom. The orange and green creature was still in the cage. It was standing on all three legs. Jake looked at it. Suddenly Jake understood something. The thing looked at Jake as if it were hungry.

5

The boys stood around Wilbur as he talked to someone at New World Bio-Laboratories. Wilbur said he was one of the students from Remsen High School who had visited the company the week before. He told the
5 person he had some questions because he was working on a project for school. Jake and the others heard the questions that Wilbur asked, but did not understand many of them. Wilbur was very intelligent, but in Biology he was even smarter than most teachers. He
10 talked for about ten minutes.

Wilbur put down the telephone and the others began asking questions all at once.

"Wait a minute," Wilbur said, holding up his hand to quiet them. "Let's go back down to the kitchen and
15 I will explain." He walked quickly down the stairs with the others hurrying behind him.

They sat around the kitchen table once again and Wilbur began to tell what he had heard. "New World was doing experiments with insects," he began. "They
20 told us that when we were there. I asked the man if they were working with spiders and ladybugs, because that thing upstairs looks like a spider and a ladybug. He said yes they were. They were trying to develop an insect that would eat smaller, plant-eating insects."

25 "Did they develop one?" Jake asked.

"The man said no. He said it would be at least five years before they would even be close. Genetic engineering is still very new. He said they just don't know enough yet," Wilbur answered.

30 "So they have not crossed a spider and a ladybug or

anything like that yet?" Joe asked.

"They don't 'cross' two animals. They take qualities from the cells of living beings and..." Wilbur explained some things to them, but he might as well have been speaking a foreign language, because none of them understood a word. 5

Jake interrupted him. "Have they developed some new form of life?"

"They could have created something they don't know about," Wilbur said. "The man told me that New World was trying to do something with ladybugs and spiders. He said they tried to *cultivate* new *beings* in seven experiments, but none of them worked." 10

"That's it," Robert exclaimed. "There are six of us and Jim Murphy makes seven." 15

"Yes," Wilbur said. "And the man said they did the work in the room we were in. He said all seven were destroyed one week before we were there."

"But they weren't," Leo said.

"No," Wilbur said. "Now we have to find a way to kill them. If we can." 20

"We could just go up and hit it with a big book or something like that," Bobby said. "Then we could go and get the other ones, at my house and all of your houses." 25

"We could do that, but we don't know what that green thing will do," said Jake. "It could jump out and maybe hurt us."

"There is one more thing," Wilbur said. He looked very worried. "When we were at New World they 30

---

cultivate, to grow, for example to cultivate a plant
being, here, living thing

29

weren't working on spiders and ladybugs. They were working on a medicine to make animals grow faster. A medicine that would make a cow or a pig or a chicken get bigger, faster, so it would give more meat.
5 Remember?"

The other boys *nodded* at Wilbur. He took his glasses off and cleaned them on his shirt as he talked. "They told us that when the preparation was finished, it would make animals grow. Their bodies would be more
10 *efficient*. The food animals eat would work better. We, and animals, eat food, but not all of the food is used by our bodies. Some of it, much of it becomes *waste material*, right? But with this new preparation the animal's body would be able to use more of what was in the food, so it
15 would grow faster."

"So the work New World did with spiders and ladybugs must have got mixed with the work they were doing with a *growth medicine*. Is that what you think, Wilbur?" Jake asked.
20 "Exactly," Wilbur answered. "New World must have created some new living creature in those seven experiments. There were probably eggs that hatched and the creatures went unnoticed. Then they began working with the growth medicine and the creatures
25 must have got into that. That thing upstairs is about the same size now as Speedy was. It ate my turtle and its body grew as big as Speedy was. There's no other way to explain it."

---

nod, move the head up and down, as if to say yes
efficient, something that works or functions well
waste material, something we get rid of or throw away
growth preparation, medicine to make plants or animals grow bigger and faster

"That means it could eat another turtle and get twice as big," Joe said.

"Maybe," Wilbur answered. "The creatures used us as *cocoons*. A *caterpillar* is hatched from an egg, then it spins a cocoon and comes out as a *butterfly*. These creatures must have done the same. They chose us, boys with brown eyes, and we were their cocoons. They came out when they were ready. Only they came in contact with the growth preparation and can grow as fast as they can eat."

"Would it eat us?" Leo asked.

"Go up and put your hand in the cage, Leo. You'll find out," Bobby said.

"I wouldn't do that, Leo. Because maybe it would bite. Remember, spiders are *poisonous*," Wilbur said. "What we must do now is find a way to kill it. Opening the cage is too dangerous. We must find another way."

"I have an idea," Jake said. "You know what happens if you knock a spider into the *sink* and pour water over it. It rolls into a ball and gets washed down the *drain*. Maybe we could pour some water into the cage and kill it."

"Good idea." Wilbur said. "Let's try."

---

poisonous, something that hurts a body. A spider bites and puts in poison, which makes a person ill
sink, place where you wash dishes
drain, see vignette, page 32

caterpillar   cocoon   butterfly

Wilbur took a *pail* from under the kitchen sink and the six of them went up to Wilbur's bedroom. Wilbur ran back downstairs to get a *funnel*. He ran back into the room with the funnel in his hand. "Someone fill the pail
5 with water," he said.

"I'll do it," Joe Lamman said and went into the bathroom with the pail.

"We can make a small opening at the top of the cage and pour water through the funnel. We'll have to fill up
10 the pail a few times to get enough water in the cage," Wilbur said.

"And then we'll see what happens," Jake added.

Joe came back a minute later. Some of the water *spilled* onto the floor as he walked into the room. He
15 put the pail of water next to the cage. Wilbur went over to the cage. There was a small door on the top. He opened the door just wide enough for the small end of the funnel to fit into it. "Start pouring the water, Joe," he said. Joe lifted the pail and began to pour into the
20 funnel. The funnel filled quickly and water spilled on the floor. He poured slower, a little bit at a time. The other boys watched.

The orange-green creature moved further into the corner. Its back was against the glass. It looked as if it

---

funnel, something used to pour water from one thing into a smaller thing
spill, fall out of a glass or other container

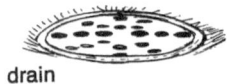

drain   pail

was pushing the glass to escape. Water dropped into the bottom of the cage.

Robert Zoe looked into the cage. With a finger he tapped the glass where the creature stood. The thing turned its head and put its open mouth against the glass 5 by Robert's finger. It's mouth looked like a *beak*. The animal's mouth opened and closed. It tried to bite through the glass to get Robert Zoe's finger. Robert

---

beak, mouth like that of a bird

pulled his hand back quickly.

Some water rolled over to the corner where the animal stood on a stone. "Somebody else pour," Joe Lamman said. "My arms are tired." Jake took the pail
5 and started to pour. When the pail was empty, Robert said: "Why don't we lift one end of the cage so the water rolls down to where the thing is?"

"Good idea," said Wilbur.

Wilbur and Jake took hold of one end of the cage.
10 "Ready?" Jake asked Wilbur. The other nodded his head. They lifted the cage slowly.

The animal in the cage made a sound when the water started to roll to that end of the cage. It sounded like the cry of a cat at night. The creature stood on one leg and
15 *clawed* at the glass with the other two. It was trying to get away from the water and escape. Its mouth bit at the glass. The top of the cage was made of wood. The boys heard a *crunch* as it bit into the wood. Another crunch and they could see its mouth coming through the wood.
20 "Hurry up!" Robert cried. "It's biting through the wood! It will get out!"

Jake and Wilbur lifted the cage higher and more water moved closer to the creature. The others watched through the glass. Water touched the animal's leg. The
25 leg seemed to *melt*. It got shorter and shorter. The animal's body moved closer to the water. It bit at the glass and its legs *waved*. The water touched its body and it got smaller. The boys saw a little bit of smoke or steam

---

claw, scratch
crunch, noise made when you bite something hard
melt, make something smaller from heat. Ice melts when heated
wave, signal (hello or goodbye) with the hand

in the cage. Finally, the animal fell into the water. Smoke came up out of the water and the animal got even smaller. Five seconds later the thing was gone. It looked as if it melted in the water, just like a piece of green-orange ice. There was nothing left.　　　　5

"It's gone," Leo said.

Jake and Wilbur put the end of the cage down. All six boys looked into the cage. There was nothing in it except stones, water, plants and the shell that once was Speedy the turtle. They looked into the cage from all 10 sides, but the animal was gone.

"The water worked," Joe said. "The thing... melted." He sounded as surprised as the others felt.

Wilbur opened the door on top of the cage. The boys could smell something bad. It smelled like *rotten* eggs. 15 Wilbur was the first to speak. "That thing's body must be made from something that reacts with water," he said. "It smells as if it burned. When it touched water it burned."

"Well, now we know how to kill them," Leo said.　　　20

"Yes," said Wilbur. "But before we kill the rest, we must find them first. We must go to all of your houses and try to kill them with water."

"My house is closest," Robert said. "Then we'll go to Bobby's, then Leo's, then to Jake's and then over to 25 your house, Joe."

"Right. Let's go," Jake said.

---

rotten, too old, for example an egg or an apple, and with a bad smell

6

It took them seven minutes to get to Robert Zoe's
house, but it felt like seven years. They ran most of
the way. Each boy felt his own fear like a live animal
crawling around inside his stomach. Nobody spoke.

5   Robert unlocked the door. They walked slowly into
the house. Their eyes moved around the room looking
into every corner. They did not know what was waiting
for them there.

"It was upstairs in the bathroom," Robert said.
10 "Let's go into the kitchen and get some water. Each of
us can carry a big glass of water, and one of us can carry
a pail."

They went to the kitchen. Robert took some glasses
from a cupboard and gave each boy one. He took a pail
15 from under the sink. Jake turned on the water and filled
his glass. Robert put the pail in the sink to fill it up. The
others put their glasses under the water and filled them
as they waited for the pail to be full.

"Ready to go," Robert said when the pail was almost
20 full. "We'll stay together. If you see the thing, throw
water on it."

They walked slowly up the stairs. Robert went first
and took the others to the bathroom. They stood
outside the door for a few seconds. "Ready?" he asked
25 the others. Nobody spoke, they only nodded their
heads.

Robert turned the doorknob and pushed the door
open. He took a step back as he did. They all looked
into the bathroom.

30   "There it is," Leo said and pointed at the window.

The green-orange thing sat by the window and looked at the boys. It was small, the same size it was when it came out of Robert's face. Leo quickly jumped forward and threw water at it. The water missed the creature, but it splashed off the window and hit the 5 thing. The boys watched as the green-orange creature got smaller and disappeared. In a second they could smell rotten eggs. It was the same smell from Wilbur's house, but not as strong.

Robert walked over to the window. Water *dripped* to 10 the floor. He moved closer to look where the animal had been. "There's something here," he said. "It looks like . . . part of a fly. It must have been eating a fly when we came in." The others came over to take a look.

"Come on," Wilbur said. "Let's go over to Bobby's 15 house. It's nearly eleven o'clock. We don't have all day." The others agreed.

They ran most of the way to Bobby's house. He lived close to Robert so it only took about two minutes. They did the same thing they had done at Wilbur's. Bobby 20 got some big glasses and he found two pails. The boys started to fill the glasses and pails with water. Bobby filled one pail. Wilbur, Jake, Leo and Robert held glasses with water in them. Water was running into Joe's pail when Bobby shouted, "THERE IT IS!" He 25 threw the water, pail and all toward Leo who stood in a corner. The water hit Leo on both legs.

"What are you doing?" Leo cried.

"It was right behind you," Bobby said. He pointed at a corner under the cupboards. "I hit it and killed it." 30

---

drip, drop in very small amounts, for example water out of a tap

"You hit me, you fool!" Leo said.

Wilbur walked over to the corner. He put his nose close to the water. "Bobby's right," he said. "I can smell it, that rotten-egg smell. He did kill it."

5 "That makes four. Now we have three more to kill," Jake said.

In twelve minutes they were at Leo Manin's house.

Leo knew something was wrong as soon as he walked into his house. "It's too quiet in here," he said. He held his head up and listened. "The bird!" Leo ran into the living room. "Oh no," he said.

Jake came up beside him and looked into the bird cage. The green-orange creature stood beside some yellow feathers. It was the size of a small bird. Jake 5 turned to the others and said: "It ate the bird."

Leo was already in the kitchen getting a glass of water. He returned to the living room. There was a dark spot on his shirt where he had spilled some water. He looked at the animal in the cage. It started to make 10 a noise and jumped at the side of the cage. The boys stepped back.

"Don't worry," Wilbur said. "It can't get out."

"How do you know?" Leo asked. "How did it get in if it can't get out?" 15

"It was small when it went in. It ate the bird and grew. Now it is too big to get out," Wilbur explained.

Leo went to the cage. He held the glass of water above the cage. The green-orange creature jumped at the top. It bit the cage. Its black legs were outside the cage, but 20 its body was too big. The thing made the same sound the other one had made. It sounded like a wild cat crying.

Leo poured some water, but the creature jumped out of the way. He tried again and moved the glass as he 25 poured. A few drops fell on the green-orange back. The creature fell to the bottom of the cage. Leo poured the rest of the water over it. In three seconds it was gone and the rotten egg smell came.

"My little sister is going to be sad," Leo said. "It was 30 her bird. She's seven years old. She will cry for days."

"You can't tell her a green and orange creature ate her bird," Wilbur said. "Let's clean up the cage and then we can leave the door open when we go. She will think it flew away. She will still be sad, but it will be better than saying the poor bird was eaten."

"You're right, Wilbur," Leo said. "Let's get going.
5 We still have two more to get."

They went over to Jake's house. Jake opened the back door and they all walked into the kitchen. The boys walked upstairs to Jake's bedroom after they each had filled a glass with water.

10 "It was under the bed," Jake told them. He got down on his hands and knees and looked under the bed. Joe and Robert went to the other side of the bed and did the same.

"Wilbur, get up on the bed and *bounce* up and down.
15 Maybe it will fall out if it is up under the bed," Jake said. Wilbur did so, but the animal was not there.

They looked everywhere in Jake's room, but could not find the animal. "We must look in the other rooms," Wilbur said. He, Robert and Jake went into
20 the bathroom. Leo, Joe and Bobby went to Jake's parents' bedroom. None of them found the creature. They went through all the rooms in the house twice. An hour and a half went by, but they found nothing.

"Where could it be?" Leo asked.

25 "I don't know," Jake said.

"The other ones we found were all near food," Wilbur said. "At my house it was in with the turtle. At Leo's it was in the bird cage. We saw part of the fly it had eaten at Robert's house. At Bobby's house we found
30 one in the kitchen. That's where there is food."

---

bounce, jump up and down

"Do you mean the food in the cupboards and refrigerator?" Jake asked.

"No, I mean living food," Wilbur said. "There are always small flies and other insects in every kitchen. So that must be why it went to Bobby's kitchen, to find 5 something to eat."

"Then let's go into the kitchen and look," Jake said.

7

The boys went to the kitchen. They stood around the table. Nobody had any good ideas about what to do.

"We have already looked here," Robert said.

"Is there any other place in the house where the
5 thing could be, Jake?" Wilbur asked. "Some place where it could find food?"

"Only here in the kitchen," Jake said. He placed his glass of water on the table and sat down. The others did the same and sat down with him. "Like you said, this
10 would be the place where there could be flies and other insects."

"We must look here again," Wilbur said. "Maybe it is somewhere else in the house. Or maybe it even went outside. But we have to look here first. He turned
15 to Jake: "Is there something I can use to clean my glasses?" he said and took his glasses off.

"Over there by the sink," Jake said and pointed.

Wilbur went over and took a paper *towel* off the roll that hung on the wall. He walked back to the table and
20 stood there cleaning his glasses while he talked. "We can start here in the kitchen," Wilbur said. "We'll look everywhere twice. It must be here. It must be." He held the glasses up to the light to see if they were clean. Then he rolled the paper into a little ball.

25 "You can throw the paper in the waste basket," Jake said. "It's over there." Jake pointed at the waste basket in the corner by the door. Wilbur walked over to the

---

towel, something used to dry dishes or the body

waste basket. There was a *swinging top* on the waste basket. The top flipped open when he stepped on the pedal. He dropped the paper towel in the basket and turned to say something to the others. Suddenly Wilbur screamed. "Help. It's biting me!"

swinging top, top that moves back and up, to open/close (on a waste paper bin)

The other boys twisted in their seats. The green-orange creature was on Wilbur's right hand. It was just a little bit bigger than it had been when it came out of Jake's face. Wilbur screamed in pain and tried to shake 5 the creature off his hand.

Jake took his glass of water from the table and threw it at Wilbur's hand. He missed. The water hit the wall. Wilbur held his hand out in front of him. He screamed for them to get it off.

10 Joe and Robert threw their water at the animal at the same time. Joe's hit it. The green-orange thing flew off with the water and disappeared. There was the smell of rotten eggs.

Wilbur held his right hand with the other hand. 15 "Oh, it hurt. The thing bit me. It hurt so much," he cried. Jake looked at Wilbur's hand. There was a little red mark, but no blood. "How does it feel now?" Jake asked him.

"It doesn't hurt any more. I can't feel my hand," 20 Wilbur said. "It feels *numb*, the way your mouth feels when you go to the dentist."

"Sit down, here," Robert said to him and pulled out a chair. Wilbur sat in the chair and rubbed his hand.

"Now we know that those things can bite," Leo said. 25 "There's one more left to get. Let's go over to Joe's and do it."

"Yes, let's go," Robert said.

"Come on," said Robert.

"I was just thinking . . ." Joe started to say. He looked 30 afraid. "We have a . . ." Joe didn't get a chance to finish

---

numb, without any feeling

what he wanted to say. There was a loud *BUMP.* Wilbur
fell off the chair and lay on the floor.

"Wilbur!" Jake cried. "What happened?" Wilbur
did not respond. His eyes rolled back in his head and his
mouth fell open. Jake got down on the floor beside him.   5
He lifted his head. "Wilbur. Wilbur," Jake said.
Wilbur's eyes were open, but he did not answer. Joe
filled a glass with water and came over to where Jake
held Wilbur. "Let me pour some water on his face," Joe
said. "Maybe that will wake him up."   10

He poured water on Wilbur's head and cheeks, but
the boy did not move.

"What do we do?" Joe asked.

"We must get him to a hospital. His heart is still
beating, but it is very slow," Jake said. His hand was on   15
Wilbur's chest. "I'll call an ambulance." He jumped
up and went to the phone. Jake pushed 911 and told
them to send an ambulance right away.

The other boys were *kneeling* around Wilbur, who lay
on the floor without moving. It did not look as if he was   20
breathing. Joe had Wilbur's head on his *lap* and was
slapping his cheeks. Wilbur did not move.

"The ambulance will be here in five minutes," Jake
said.

"Will he be all right? He isn't going to die, is he?"   25
Robert asked.

"I don't know," Jake answered. "I hope he will be all
right." He looked down at Wilbur. His eyes were open,
but only the whites showed. Jake saw Wilbur's chest

---

bump, a loud noise
kneel, sit on your knees
lap, the top of the legs when one sits down

45

going slowly up and down. It was the only sign that the boy was still alive.

"What will we say when the ambulance gets here?" Leo asked. "We can't say he was bitten by a green and orange animal that jumped out of someone's face. Nobody would believe that."

"You're right," Robert said. "What can we say?"

"Let's just say he was bitten by a spider," Bobby suggested. "That's almost the truth."

"Good idea," Jake said. "Someone must go to the hospital with him."

"And don't forget we have to go over to Joe's house and get the last one," Bobby reminded them.

Jake thought for a few seconds. "I have an idea," he said. He went over to the cupboard and took out a pencil and paper. He tore a piece of paper into four smaller pieces. Jake wrote something on all four pieces of paper. Then he folded each one twice.

"I've written two J's and two H's on the papers," he said and held out his hand. "Each of you take one. Joe and the J's go to Joe's and the H's will go to the hospital with Wilbur."

Each boy took a paper from Jake's hand. They opened them slowly.

"I got a J," Robert said.

"H here," said Leo.

"I got an H too," said Bobby.

Jake opened his and showed the others the J that was written there. "Bobby and Leo will go to the hospital then. Robert and I will go with Joe over to his house and try to get the last one."

The doorbell rang. Jake hurried to the door and opened it. Two men in white clothes walked in with a *stretcher.* Jake led them into the kitchen. They began to put Wilbur onto the stretcher.

"What happened?" one of the men asked when he saw Wilbur on the floor. He got to his knees and put a finger on Wilbur's throat to feel if there was a *heartbeat.* 5 None of the boys spoke for a few seconds. Finally Bobby said: "He ah.. a spider bit him."

"When did it happen?" the man asked.

"Just about ten minutes ago," Bobby answered.

"What kind of spider was it?" the other man asked 10 Bobby.

Bobby did not know what to say. He looked to the other boys for an answer. Nobody spoke for a few seconds.

"We don't know," Bobby said. 15

"Where is the spider. Is it alive?" the man asked.

"No, it's dead. We killed it and washed it down the sink," Jake said.

"You should have saved it. Then the doctors could see what kind of medicine to use," the man said. He 20 turned to his partner. "Are you ready?" The other said he was and they lifted the stretcher.

"Does he live here?"

"No, I do," Jake answered.

"Somebody should call this boy's parents." 25

"Can two of us go with you?" Bobby asked. "Then we can call his parents from the hospital." The man said they could.

---

stretcher, something like a bed to carry a sick person
heartbeat, the sound the heart makes

The two men put Wilbur into the back of the ambulance. Bobby and Leo got in beside him. The ambulance drove away with the *siren screeching* and blue lights flashing. Joe, Robert and Jake ran off toward
5 Joe's house.

---

siren, something on a police car, fire truck or ambulance that makes a high loud noise
screech, high loud noise, like the siren

8

Robert, Jake and Joe ran for several minutes before slowing down. They walked for a minute or two to catch their breaths and then started to run agin. Joe lived about two kilometers from Jake and they wanted to get there fast. His house was close to their school, so they had to take the long way around to get to Joe's. They didn't want anybody from school to see them.　　10

Robert and Jake talked as they walked and ran. Most of what they talked about was Wilbur. Would he be all right? What would the doctors say at the hospital? There were many questions and they had none of the answers. Joe did not say much as they went. Robert and　15
Jake did most of the talking.

In fifteen minutes they were in front of Joe's house. Jake said: "Let's go in and get the last one. Then we can go over to the hospital and see how Wilbur is."

Joe looked down at the ground and said: "I've been　20
thinking . . . no . . . it couldn't be."

"What?" Robert asked.

"I was just thinking," Joe answered. "We have a dog. Could it . . . no that's a silly idea."

"Do you mean, could it eat your dog?" Jake asked.　25

"Yes, do you think it could?"

"No, that's impossible," Robert said. "A dog is just too big and too smart."

"Yes, a dog is too big," Jake said. "What kind of dog do you have?"

"A Golden Retriever."

"That's a very big dog," Robert said. "Don't worry.

Dogs are smart. They can *sense* danger and know enough to stay away from it."

"But why did it bite Wilbur?" Joe asked.

"It probably bit him because his hand was in the waste basket," Jake said. "Spiders bite and they don't eat you."

"Yes, but some spiders put poison into the flies and insects they catch. Then the insect can't move," Joe said. "And they eat them."

"It couldn't eat a dog, Joe. A turtle, a fly or a bird, yes. But not a dog," Jake said. "The things tried to bite us and bit Wilbur because they were afraid. They were trying to protect their lives. That must be the reason why. Not because they wanted to eat Wilbur, or any of us. They were probably just afraid we would hurt them."

"Come on, let's go," Robert said. He put his hand on Joe's shoulder. "Come on, Joe. We'll get this last one and get over to the hospital."

Joe nodded his head and they walked to the front door. The other two watched as Joe took out his key and put it in the door. He turned the key with a *click*, took it out and put it back in his pocket. Joe turned the *doorknob* and opened the door a little. Jake stood on his toes and looked over Joe's shoulder. Robert did the same.

Joe started to step into the house and stopped. He screamed in terror. Jake noticed the same thing Joe saw. There was the *skeleton* of a dog on the floor about

---

sense, feel
click, sharp sound
doorknob, handle used to open and close a door
skeleton, bones inside an animal or person

eight steps ahead of them. Nothing was left of the
Golden Retriever except the *bare* bones. What once was
the dog's head was now a *skull*. It lay on the floor and
seemed to look at them with empty eyes and a terrifying
smile.   5

Jake grabbed Joe's shoulder just as he tried to push
in the door. Jake pulled him back and *slammed* the door
shut. BOOM! Something banged hard against the
door from the inside.

"Oh no! Oh no!," Joe cried. "I'll kill it. That thing   10
killed Lucky." He turned his back to the others so they
would not see him crying.

"What was that noise?" Robert asked. He knew
what made the noise but could not say it. Jake and
Joe knew what had banged against the door. Their   15
pounding hearts understood, but their minds refused
to believe it.

"It did eat the dog. Now it's as big as a dog and it
wants to get us," Jake whispered so Joe could not hear
him.   20

"It can't be," Robert said.

"I saw the skeleton of the dog on the floor," Jake said.
"Joe saw it too."

Robert looked at Joe then back to Jake. He knew
Jake was telling the truth.   25

"What are we going to do?" Robert asked.

"Just what we came over here to do," Joe answered,
as he came toward them. "Kill it the same way we did
the others."

---

bare, naked: with nothing over it
skull, bone at the top of the head
slammed, hit against something hard

Jake walked over to a window. He got down low and moved his head up slowly. The others came over to the window and did the same. They saw the green-orange creature standing on a little table in Joe's living room.
5 It stood on two legs and rubbed the third leg over its head, like a fly does. It was as big as a large dog. The head moved in a circle. The creature's eyes were like black tennis balls.

The boys *backed away* from the window. "How can we
10 do it?" Jake asked. "Is there any water outside."

"Do you think we can kill it with water?" Robert asked. "It's so big."

"We have to try," Jake said. "Water killed the other ones. I hope it will kill this one."

15 "I've got a good idea," Joe said. "There's a garden *hose* at the side of the house. We can use that." He ran around the side of the house. Jake and Robert followed him.

A garden hose hung next to a water *faucet* on the side
20 of the house. Joe dropped to his knees. He took the hose off its hook and let it fall on the grass. Jake picked up the end of the hose and Joe turned on the faucet. Water *sprayed out* over the grass. Jake turned the top to stop the flow of water. Robert took the rest of the hose and
25 started to unroll it.

"Let's go," Joe said. His voice was just a frightened whisper. The three walked around the house toward the front door again. Robert unrolled the hose as they

---

back away, move away backwards
hose, tube used to direct water at something
faucet, thing you open to get water in a house
spray out, come out in many directions

walked. When they were at the door, Joe said: "Give me the hose, Jake. I want to get that thing."

"I can do it," Jake said.

"No, it's my house and it was my dog. I'll do it."

Jake handed the end of the hose to Joe and said, 5 "OK. I'll get the door."

"What if the water doesn't kill it. What if the thing is too big and the water doesn't work?" Robert asked.

Jake stepped up to the door. "If it doesn't work, then...it doesn't work," he said. Jake tried not to 10 think what would happen if the water did not kill the creature. "But we must try." He turned to Joe and asked: "Are you ready?" Joe said he was. "Robert, if something happens to Joe or me, you must take over. That thing in there is dangerous and we must kill it." 15 Robert nodded his head.

Jake put his hand on the doorknob and slowly turned it. He pushed the door open a couple of centimeters. Joe stood behind him ready to turn on the water. Jake opened the door a couple of more centimeters. 20

Suddenly, the green-orange creature jumped at the door. One black leg landed on Jake's arm. It felt like a long hairy *snake*. The leg bent and started to squeeze Jake's arm.

snake

The creature's mouth was in the door opening. It snapped like a giant scissors. Jake screamed and pulled the door closed. The hairy leg hung outside the door. It moved up, down and around as it tried to grab something. They could hear the creature scraping at the inside of the door with its other legs. 5

Joe twisted the head of the hose and water shot out. He pointed at the leg and hit it in the middle. The hairy black leg broke in two. Half of the leg melted and the other half fell to the ground. There was a BOOM 10 from inside, as the thing's body broke from the leg and fell to the floor. The piece of leg on the ground still moved. Joe sprayed water on it and the leg disappeared. They heard a loud THUD. The door shook as the creature jumped against it. 15

"That was close, too close," Jake said. "But we can't stop now."

"Jake, open the door fast and I'll try to get it," Joe said. He turned on the water so it splashed against the door. Jake stepped up to the door. Water splashed into 20 his face as he turned the knob. There was a BOOM as the thing hit the door. Jake pushed the door open and jumped back.

The green-orange creature jumped through the door. Its mouth was wide open. Joe pointed the flow of 25 water at the creature flying toward him. He hit it right in the middle. It fell to the ground and rolled over. It howled like a wild cat. The mouth snapped open and closed as it tried to bite anything it could. Joe continued to spray water on the green-orange creature. It got 30 smaller and smaller. Finally it was gone and all that was left was the terrible smell of rotten eggs. The smell was so bad the boys had to turn their heads to get air.

Joe held the spray of water on the spot where the thing had been. There was hate in his eyes; hate for the creature that killed his dog. Jake had to stop him. "It's dead, Joe," he said. "It's over now." Joe *screwed* the top
5 of the hose and the water stopped, but tears continued to flow from his eyes. The three boys looked at each other, but could not speak. It felt as if a nightmare had just ended.

"Let's clean up the water in the house and get over to
10 the hospital," Jake said.

Joe and Jake dried the water while Robert put the hose back in place. Joe stood over the bones that lay on the floor. "We can bury Lucky in the garden," he said and another tear rolled down his cheek.

15 "What will you tell your parents?" Joe asked him.

"I don't know," Robert answered. "I just don't know."

They buried Lucky behind the house and started off toward the hospital.

---

screw, turn to open or close something

9

Bobby and Leo sat beside Wilbur's bed in Remsen General Hospital. Joe, Robert and Jake walked into the room and were surprised to see Wilbur sitting up in bed. "Wilbur?" Jake said as he walked into the room.

"Hi Jake," he answered. 5

"Are you all right?" Robert asked.

"My head hurts a little bit, but otherwise I feel all right," Wilbur answered. "The doctor gave me medicine against spider bites and I guess it worked. When I was on the floor at your house, Jake, I couldn't move. I 10 couldn't even feel my body. But I could think and hear what you all said. I've never been so afraid in my life. I thought I was going to die."

"Well you're all right now, Wilbur," Bobby said. "And the doctor said you can go home." 15

"You can go home now?" Robert asked.

"Yes, the doctor said I could. If there are any problems I should call the hospital, but I don't think there will be any problems."

The boys sat and talked for about half an hour. Jake, 20 Joe and Robert told about how they had killed the final creature at Joe's house. The other three listened and could hardly believe it, but they knew it was the truth.

"What are we going to tell people," Leo asked them all. 25

"We don't have to tell them anything," Wilbur said. "We are the only one's who saw the creatures."

"We must tell somebody," Joe said. "Maybe there are more experiments and more companies making mistakes... and making new things that are dan- 30

gerous."

"What about New World? Should we call them and tell them?" Bobby asked.

"We should, but we cannot. For one thing, New

World would *deny* the whole story. They would say it was not true," Wilbur explained.

"But we saw them. We know it happened," Robert exclaimed.

"We saw them, yes. But we don't have any proof," 5 Wilbur said. "If we tried to tell the story to a newspaper, we would get into trouble. It's our word against New World's and that is a big company. Who would believe us?"

"Maybe some day we can tell somebody," Jake said. 10 "I wish that companies like New World would be more careful in the future. If only we could stop them. Maybe we could write them a letter and tell what happened."

"We would still have to prove it," Wilbur said. "And we can't. They would throw the letter away." 15

"What about Jim Murphy. He must be in trouble," Joe said.

"No, I called his house. He told his parents some kind of insect jumped onto his face and scared him. He said if he told them it jumped out of his cheek, they 20 wouldn't believe it," Bobby told them. "His parents believed him when he told them he didn't use drugs. I told him our story too. That made him feel a little bit better, but he could hardly believe one of the creatures ate a turtle." 25

Wilbur's mother stopped the conversation when she walked into the room. She sat at Wilbur's side and talked to him for a few minutes. The others stood around, but had little to say.

Five minutes later a nurse walked into the room. She 30

---

deny, say you haven't done something

told Wilbur he could go home. Wilbur's mother asked them if they wanted a ride, but they all said no. The boys left the hospital and walked together for a while. Then they split up to go to their own homes. Bobby and
5 Jake went together to the corner of Elm and High streets and then split up.

Jake's mother was already home when he got there. She *scolded* him again when she saw the little red + on his cheek. "I told you not to squeeze that pimple.
10 Now you have a red mark." His father came several minutes later.

At six o'clock the family sat down to dinner. Jake was not very hungry after all the horrors of the day. "Why aren't you eating your peas and carrots, Jake?" his
15 mother asked.

Jake looked down at the peas and carrots on his plate. It reminded him of the green-orange creatures. His stomach turned. "I'm not very hungry, Mom."

The next day in school, the six boys and Jim Murphy
20 met before they went into Biology class. "What did you tell your parents, Joe?" Wilbur asked.

"I told them I found the dog in the street. I said it had been hit by a car," Joe answered. "And I told them we buried the dog behind the house." He looked away from
25 the other boys and wiped his eyes.

"Did they believe you?" Robert wanted to know.

Joe waited a few seconds before answering. "My father wanted to call the police, to find the driver of the car," he began. "But my mother said they could never

---

scold, tell somebody what they did wrong, and not to do it again

60

find him. She said we ought to get a new dog."

"What about your bird, Leo?" Jake asked.

"I told them it must have flown out of the house," Leo answered. "It was sad. My little sister stayed outside until eight o'clock. She looked everywhere and 5 waited for the bird to come home. Finally I promised her I would buy her a new one. She was still crying when I left for school."

The boys agreed they would never tell anybody about what happened for at least five years. Joe said, 10 "Five minutes or five years, nobody would believe us anyway." They all shook hands with each other and promised not to say a word about it for five years. The bell rang and they went to class.

Suzy Monohan sat at the desk beside Jake and said: 15 "Hi." Jake said hello. "I didn't see you after Biology class yesterday."

"No, I ah . . . .." Just then Mr Damick walked into the room. He held a piece of paper in his hand. "There are a few young men here who seem to think there are some 20 things that are more interesting than school," he said. He read from the paper. "The following boys will report to the office right now: Jake Winslow, Bobby Rockla, Joe Lamman, Robert Zoe, Leo Manin and . . . Wilbur Ericsson." It sounded like a question 25 when he said Wilbur's name.

Jim Murphy watched as the six left the room. Jake turned his head and nodded at Jim, who returned the signal. On the way to the office Wilbur said: "I've never been in trouble before." He sounded worried. 30

"Don't worry, Wilbur," Leo Manin said. "I've been to the office a hundred times. They talk to you, make you promise never to do it again and then let you go."

In the office, the principal stood them up in a line and asked: "Where were you boys yesterday?" Nobody said a word. Then Wilbur said: "We were working on a project about New World Bio Laboratories for Biology
5 class." He looked the principal right in the eye when he said it. The principal talked to them for about three minutes. He told them how wrong it was to *skip* school and made them promise never to do it again.

When they were out in the hall, Jake turned to
10 Wilbur and said "Maybe you've never been in trouble before, but you're pretty good at it."

Questions

How would you react if an insect came out of your body?

What should the boys do? Tell their parents, the police or New World? What would you do?

Jake's mother told him not to squeeze the pimple. How much should a parent have to say about how a teenager looks, dresses, uses make-up?

How would you react if a student in your class was accused of using drugs and you knew that he or she never touched drugs at all?

Is bio-technology a good thing? What things does it, and genetic engineering, produce?

Should genetic engineering be allowed? Should it be controlled? Give examples of how.

Is what happened in the story possible, do you think? Or will it be possible in the future?

Which of the boys did you like the best and why?

Do you think Wilbur will continue to be a friend of the other boys? Why? Why not?

What could have happened, if one of the green-orange creatures had lived?

Have you ever seen or experiemced anything that you could not understand; an UFO, ghost, etc.?

TEEN READERS NOW AVAILABLE:

Find all titles at **easyreaders.eu**.